D1158159

JUV
F
2161
.E913
1995

EXQUEMELIN AND THE PIRATES OF THE CARIBBEAN

HISTORY EYEWITNESS

EDITED WITH AN INTRODUCTION
AND ADDITIONAL MATERIAL BY
JANE SHUTER

RSVP
**RAINTREE
STECK-VAUGHN**
PUBLISHERS
The Steck-Vaughn Company

Austin, Texas

HUNTSVILLE PUBLIC LIBRARY
HUNTSVILLE, TEXAS 77340

065981

© Copyright 1995, text, Steck-Vaughn Company

All rights reserved. No part of this book may be reproduced
or utilized in any form or by any means, electronic or mechanical,
including photocopying, recording, or by any information storage
and retrieval system, without permission in writing from the
Publisher. Inquiries should be addressed to: Copyright
Permissions, Steck-Vaughn Company, P.O. Box 26015,
Austin, TX 78755

Published by Raintree Steck-Vaughn Publishers, an
imprint of Steck-Vaughn Company

Design by Saffron House, map by Jeff Edwards.

Library of Congress Cataloging-in-Publication Data

Exquemelin, A. O. (Alexandre Oliver)
    Exquemelin and the pirates of the Caribbean / edited with
    an introduction and additional material by Jane Shuter.
        p.   cm. — (History eyewitness)
    Includes index.
    ISBN 0-8114-8282-0
    1. Buccaneers — Juvenile literature.   2. Pirates —
Caribbean Area — History — 17th century — Juvenile litera-
ture.   3. Spanish Main — Juvenile literature.   4. Caribbean
Area — History — To 1810 — Juvenile literature.
5. Exquemelin, A. O. (Alexandre Olivier) [1. Buccaneers.
2. Pirates. 3. Spanish Main.] I. Shuter, Jane. II. Title.
III. Series.
F2161.E913   1995
972.9'03—dc20   94-28702
[B]   CIP   AC

Printed in China
Bound in the United States

1 2 3 4 5 6 7 8 9 0   99 98 97 96 95 94

Acknowledgments

The publishers would like to thank the following for
permission to reproduce photographs:

Bettman Archive: p.12
British Library: p.32
British Museum: p.18, p.20, p.45
CAA/Gibbes Museum of Art: p.10
e t archive: p.8
Hubert Josse: p.7
Mansell Collection: p.39
Robert Marx: p.22, p.29, p.30, p.36, p.43
Dr Peter Marsden: cover and p.16
Peter Newark: p.35
Newport Borough Council: p.24
North Wind Picture Archives: cover
Planet Earth Pictures: p.14, p.43

Every effort has been made to contact copyright holders of material
reproduced in this book. Any omissions will be rectified in
subsequent printings if notice is given to the publisher.

Note to the Reader

In this book some of the words are printed in **bold** type. This indicates that the
word is listed in the glossary on pages 46–47. The glossary gives a brief explana-
tion of words that may be new to you.

CONTENTS

Introduction

Exquemelin is a shadowy figure. Most of what we know about him comes from his writings, or the introductions to the various editions of his book. He was probably born in France about 1654 and left for Tortuga, in the West Indies, on a French trading ship as an **indentured servant** of the French **West India Company**. He was sold when the company collapsed. His first master, the Deputy Governor of Tortuga, treated him badly. He was sold to a doctor, who eventually let him buy his freedom. He then joined the **pirates**, probably as a **barber surgeon**. He returned to Europe to live in Holland and is listed as having passed the examinations of the Dutch Surgeons' Guild in 1679. He returned to the West Indies as a ship's surgeon in the Battle of Cartagena in 1697, the last big battle the pirates fought. This is the last we hear of him.

The pirates of the West Indies started as hunters. They were people who had left the Spanish-controlled mainland of South America for various reasons. From 1610 onward they lived on the island of Hispaniola (now Haiti), chosen because it was uninhabited. The previous inhabitants had been driven out by the Spanish, but they left behind cattle and pigs, which bred rapidly and ran wild. The new settlers hunted these animals. They lived by selling the **hides** and also the meat, which they dried over open fires called *boucans*. This is how they got the name **buccaneers.** The Spanish kept trying to break up the buccaneers, because they did not obey the Spanish laws, but had their own rules called the **Customs of the Coast**. Finally the Spanish killed off most of the animals on Hispaniola, thinking this would finish the buccaneers. Instead they moved to the nearby island of Tortuga and turned to piracy. They began by attacking in **dug-out canoes,** with only **muskets** for weapons. They soon had better ships and weapons—those they captured. Between 1655 and 1671 the buccaneers flourished. Exquemelin sailed with them from 1666 to 1674. They attacked any ship they chose, and they all worked together. Then the English and French governors on the islands off the coast of South America began to pay the pirates to fight the Spanish. The pirates worked more and more for one country, recruited mostly their fellow countrymen, and at last excluded, and even fought, buccaneers of other nations. As soon as they stopped working as a group, they were doomed.

Exquemelin's book was written in Dutch and then was printed in several editions in several languages. This book is edited from the first English edition, published in 1684 by William Crook. It is difficult to know how accurate Exquemelin's writings are. They could be fictitious, as we know so little about him. However, historians have checked his references to events and people and found that he is quite accurate, although sometimes a bit confused about his dates.

INDENTURED SERVANTS

These were people who signed an agreement to work for a person or a company for a number of years in return for free transport to another country. Often this was the only way that poorer people could afford to emigrate. However, this agreement had the disadvantage that a person's service was seen as a piece of property. It could be sold to other people without consultation. Many people sold their servants' indentures as soon as they landed. Being an indentured servant was a form of voluntary slavery, but slavery with conditions that the employer was supposed to abide by. In reality there was no way of enforcing the conditions of work.

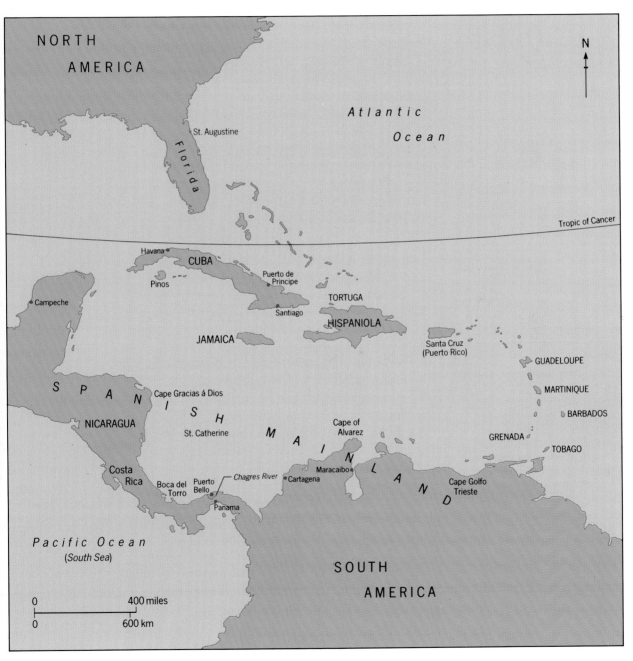

The Caribbean islands and Spanish-controlled South American mainland in the 1660s. This map shows some of the places Exquemelin mentions in his book.

NORTH AMERICA

Atlantic Ocean

N

St. Augustine

Florida

Tropic of Cancer

Havana
CUBA
Pinos
Puerto de Principe
Campeche
Santiago
TORTUGA
HISPANIOLA
JAMAICA
Santa Cruz (Puerto Rico)
GUADELOUPE
MARTINIQUE
BARBADOS

S P A N I S H   M A I N L A N D

Cape Gracias á Dios
NICARAGUA
St. Catherine
Cape of Alvarez
GRENADA
TOBAGO
Costa Rica
Boca del Torro
Puerto Bello
Chagres River
Cartagena
Maracaibo
Cape Golfo Trieste
Panama

Pacific Ocean
(South Sea)

SOUTH AMERICA

0   400 miles
0   600 km

CHAPTER 1

Sailing to the Caribbean

We set sail from France in a ship called the *St. John* on May 2, 1666. The ship carried 28 guns and 20 seamen, as well as 220 passengers, including indentured servants (who were sent as free passengers by the West India Company, for they were to work for the Company) and free persons with their servants. We then anchored to wait for seven more of the Company's ships due from Dieppe. These were traveling with a warship carrying 37 guns and 250 men. We were joined by other ships, making about 30 **sail** in all. We set sail in a good defensive formation, fearing an English attack. There was a good wind and foggy weather, which stopped the English from sighting us. We kept close to the French coast to avoid them, stopping to take on **provisions** and **fresh water.** We took a longer route for fear of attack by the English ships that were cruising thereabouts to meet us.

We had good weather until Cape Finisterre. Here a very heavy storm separated us from the rest. This storm lasted eight days. It was pitiful to see how miserably the passengers were tumbled to and fro, on all sides of the ship; the sailors had to step over them to do their work. Afterward we had good winds until we came to the **Tropic of Cancer.** Here we also had **favorable winds,** which we badly needed, for we were running short of water, being each **rationed** to a pint a day. About the latitude of Barbados, we met an English ship, which gave chase, but seeing he could not catch us, he drew off. We then chased him, firing on him with our **eight pounders,** but he was better **rigged** and at length escaped. We then resumed our course. Not long after, we sighted the island of Martinique. We tried to reach the coast of the island of St. Peter but were prevented by a storm. We then steered for the island of Guadeloupe but could not reach this island because of the same storm, so we carried on to the island of Tortuga, which was our eventual destination. We reached Tortuga on July 7, 1666, without having lost a man on the whole voyage. We unloaded the goods that belonged to the Company of the West Indies; and soon after, the ship was sent to **Cul de Sac** with some passengers.

THE DANGERS OF TRAVEL

Sea voyages were never safe. Even in times of peace, they were made more dangerous by the possibility of attack by ships from other countries. Because groups of ships were less likely to be attacked, captains tried to travel with other ships from a friendly country as much as possible. They were prepared to use longer routes to avoid meeting ships from rival countries. Even trading ships were armed: the *St. John* had 28 cannons.

This painting shows a variety of French ships in the port of Amsterdam about 1660. All but the row boat in the foreground would have been seagoing. The two largest ships are frigates.

CHAPTER 2

Life in the Caribbean

Tortuga is on the north side of Hispaniola, near South America. The Spanish named this island after the shape of the land, which resembles a great **sea tortoise**, called by them *Tortuga de mar*.

The land is very mountainous and rocky, but even so huge leafy trees grow there, their roots all entangled in the rocks, like ivy on a wall. The north of the island is totally uninhabited. First, it has proved to be unhealthy, and second, the ruggedness of the coast gives no access to the shore, unless across the rocks. So the island is populated only in

A lande Crab.

the south, which has one good port with two channels of entry and room for many ships. The inhabited area is divided into four parts of which the first is the Low Land, or Low Country. This part is the most important, because it has the port, Cayona. This is where the richest **planters** on the island live. The second part is called the Middle Plantation. Its soil is hardly used and is good for growing tobacco. The third is called Ringot. These places are on the western side of the island. The fourth, and last, is called The Mountain, where the first plantations were established.

As to the wood that grows on the island, we have already said that the trees are exceedingly tall; they are also useful. There is the candlewood tree, which burns brightly, like a candle, and which they use for their night fishing. There is also *Lignum sanctum,* which has medicinal uses, and other medicinal herbs. Also there is China root, but this is too white and soft to be of much use. The wild boars eat it if they can find nothing else. The wood is used for shipbuilding and house building, too. There are many fruits, of which I shall name only the most common. There are the **manioc** (cassava), **yams,** melons and watermelons, bananas, pineapples, and cashew nuts. There are also palm trees. Their juice is used for wine, and their leaves are used instead of tiles to roof the houses. There are also wild boar. The Governor has forbidden hunting them with dogs, for fear of killing them all off. There are wild pigeons, which can be eaten. On the seashores there are many land and sea crabs—both kinds are very large. These are good to feed to the servants and slaves, who find them very tasty. They are bad for the sight. When eaten too often, they cause great giddiness in the head and a weakness of the brain; people cannot see for around a quarter of an hour.

This is a crab of the kind described by Exquemelin. It was painted by John White in 1585. It is uncertain why the crab meat affected people in the way described by Exquemelin.

SETTLING THE WEST INDIES

Spain had been granted most of South America by the Pope in 1494 and so controlled much of the trade in the area. However, other countries were able to set up trading posts on the Caribbean islands. They were able to become involved in the profitable slave trade, and the trade in spices, tobacco, and sugar. They were also able to attack the Spanish ships that carried gold from South America back to Spain.

CHAPTER 3

Growing Tobacco

PLANTATIONS
Planters were often the first people to settle the islands of the Caribbean, although Exquemelin claims that in Tortuga they were outnumbered by hunters and pirates at first. Planters had a hard life. First, they had to find a place to settle that was close to a fresh water supply. They had to clear the land and build homes. The land was then cleared for the crops and the soil broken up, ready for planting. Then they had to decide which crops to grow. This was a gamble, for some crops, such as sugar, would grow well on one island but fail completely on another. Very few planters made much of a living. It was no wonder that many of them turned to piracy instead.

The planters began to cultivate Tortuga in 1598. Tobacco was their main crop, although there was not much land to grow it on. They tried to plant sugar, but it was too costly a venture. The island had more hunters and pirates than planters, to begin with. When the laws against hunting came, many hunters tried growing tobacco in the area called Cul de Sac, in the south. They cleared the ground in groups, chopping down trees and rooting up shrubs, until they had cleared enough land for everyone in the group. The first crop on this new land was a bean crop, which grew and was picked within six weeks. Then they planted potatoes, which took four or five months to grow and mature. They eat these cooked in boiling water and also make a drink from them, which they were taught to make by the Indians. They then grew manioc, which took almost a year to come to perfection. From it they make a flour for bread, as wheat will not grow here. It is a thin, **unleaven** bread; they make it in batches and dry it on the roofs of their houses. Any that start to rot are used to make a drink that is like beer. They grow bananas, too, and a drink can be made from these. But it easily causes drunkenness, and if too much is drunk, it inflames the throat.

Once these plants are established, some of the land can be set aside to grow tobacco for trade. They make beds of earth, no larger than 12 feet square [1.1 square meters.] They sow the tobacco and cover the bed with palm leaves to keep out the sunlight. They water the soil when it does not rain, as we do our gardens in Europe. When it is about the size of a small lettuce, they transplant it into a bigger field, in rows, each plant 3 feet [1 meter] from the other. The best season, when the most rains fall, is January to March. They need to weed the soil very carefully. When the plants are about a foot and a half [half a

meter] high, they cut off the tops to stop them from shooting up, and to nourish the already established leaves. As the tobacco matures, they build huts 50–60 feet [18 meters] long and 30–40 feet [12 meters] wide. They fill them with branches on which the tobacco leaves are dried. When they are dry, the leaves are stripped from the stalks and rolled by people who do only this job, who are paid by one-tenth of what they have rolled. When picked, the leaves will sprout again several times. The planters prospered; there are now about 200 planters there.

An early tobacco plantation. Methods of growing and preparing tobacco were still almost the same over a hundred years later, as we discover from the descriptions by American slaves of their work on tobacco plantations in North America. The huts in the picture are built of bricks, whereas the ones on Tortuga were more likely to have been made of wood thatched with palm leaves.

CHAPTER 4

Slaves

THE SLAVE TRADE

Slaves were being used in America almost as soon as European settlement began. In 1562 John Hawkins, a famous English explorer, made his first successful trading expedition. He bought native Africans and then sailed to the West Indies. There he sold them as slaves to the Spanish on the mainland and with the proceeds of the sale bought pearls, sugar, and gold. The system of sailing from Britain with pots and pans and cloth, selling them in Africa for slaves, and trading the slaves in America for luxuries such as tobacco and sugar became known as the Triangular Trade (because of the shape made by the route the ships took). This system continued until the slave trade was abolished by Britain in 1807. Many trading families made huge fortunes from the slave trade.

In this country the planters have very few **slaves.** Because of this they themselves, and some servants, have to do much of the **drudgery.** The servants bind themselves to their masters for three years. But the masters, ignoring their consciences, often sell them, like horses at a **fair.** They sell them just as they sell what Negroes they can get, which are brought to them from the coast of Guinea [in Africa]. Indeed, when people from these islands go back to the countries in Europe, they often collect young men and boys, by fair promises and even kidnapping, and then bring them back and force them to work like horses.

The work they give these Europeans and the other indentured servants is often harder even than that they give the Negroes, their slaves. They take more care of the slaves, for they have paid for them, and they are bound to their masters for life. The white servants

The slaves on the left are treating manioc to make it into flour. The slaves on the right are processing tobacco leaves. The circular shapes on the roofs of the huts are the flat loaves of bread made with manioc flour. They are being dried in the sun (see page 10).

are only to serve for three years or so; the masters do not care if they live or die. Among these, and among some of the transported people, there are many of good quality and tender education who are of a softer constitution and more prone to catching the native diseases. Even if they do not die in this way, they are often beaten so badly that they fall down dead at the feet of their cruel masters.

We were on an island called Gracias á Dios where we saw that there were Negroes living with the Indians. Two of our pirates could speak the language of the Indians, and they said the Negroes were escaped slaves. These Negroes had overcome their captors off the island and seized the ship, hoping to sail back to Africa. However, they were unable to manage to sail the ship well enough to return to their homeland, so they made their home with the Indians instead, living with them according to their customs.

HUNTSVILLE PUBLIC LIBRARY
HUNTSVILLE, TEXAS 77340

065981

CHAPTER 5

How Exquemelin Joined the Pirates

Several governors ran the island of Tortuga until 1664, when the West India Company of France took over, providing their own governor, Monsieur Ogeron. They brought over many **factors** and servants, thinking to take over and trade with other countries from there. But they could not do this; they could not even set up trade with their own people. The pirates, hunters, and planters of Tortuga promised to buy their necessities from the Company and were given them on **credit.** The Company soon found that they could not get either payment or the return of their goods from those people, not even by bringing in armed men. So the Company told their factors to sell everything that the Company owned, even the servants belonging to the Company (which were sold some for 20, others for 30, **pieces of eight**) and all other goods. I was also sold, as a servant of the said Company, in whose service I came out of France.

I was unlucky. I fell into the hands of a cruel tyrant, the Lieutenant General of the island. This man treated me cruelly; I thought I would die of hunger. He said I could buy my freedom for 300 pieces of eight, and me without a penny in the world. At last I grew very sick, and my master feared I would die. Fearing that this would mean that he had no profit from the money he had given for me, he sold me to a surgeon for 70 pieces of eight. With him I began to recover my health, as he was kind to me.

TRADING COMPANIES

Spain ruled mainland South America, but other countries sent people to settle in the Caribbean islands, to trade with the mainland and their home countries. Trading companies were often set up to share the costs and profits of the journeys. The profits could make a company very rich, like the British East India Company. But disasters such as lost ships and cargoes, or unpaid debts, could cause a company to collapse, like the French West India Company. When companies collapsed, they had to sell everything they had to try to pay their debts. In the case of the French West India Company, they even managed to sell the services of their indentured servants.

He gave me clothes and very good food, and after I had served him for just a year, he gave me my freedom, on a promise that I would pay him 100 pieces of eight as soon as I was able.

I was now free, but had nothing, and did not know how to make my living. So I decided to join the wicked order of pirates or robbers at sea. I was accepted into this society and stayed with them until 1672.

This photograph shows some of the household goods from the seventeenth century that have been discovered at the Jamaican town of Port Royal. These would probably have been brought to the islands from Europe. They would have been expensive and would have been seen as valuables, rather than just useful equipment. Plates, bowls, and cups would more usually have been made from wood. Because wood rots, there are no examples of these left today.

CHAPTER 6

Pirate Customs

Before a voyage the pirates tell everyone involved when to **embark**, and what to bring with them: so many pounds of gunpowder, and **shot** and so forth. On board they hold a council as to where to go and what provisions to get. (They eat mostly meat, and this mostly pork or turtles, which they salt down.) Sometimes their provisions are obtained by piracy. They rob **hog-yards** where the Spanish keep thousands of **swine** together. They attack by night, breaking into the keeper's lodge and forcing him to give as many as they need, on pain of death. On board ship every man is allowed as much meat as he can eat twice a day.

Once provisioned they decide where to go. They also agree on certain **articles**, which are put in writing, and all have to sign. Here they specify what each person will be paid for that voyage, taken from what they take on the whole expedition. It is the same law with these as with other pirates: *no prey, no pay*. First they decide what to pay the captain for the use of his ship and then the carpenter or shipwright who made her fit to sail. This is mostly about 100 to 150 pieces of eight. Next they allow 200 pieces of eight for provisions. Then they allow for the surgeon and his medicine chest, which is usually rated at 200 or 250 pieces of eight.

LOSING LIMBS

The compensation for loss of limbs and other parts of the body was probably seen as vital for two reasons. The first is that a pirate needed, for his trade, to be fit and healthy. The second is that an injury, except the very slightest, was likely to have extremely severe consequences. Medical supplies were limited, bad hygiene made infection very likely, and the ships' surgeons and doctors were often unqualified amateurs. Exquemelin himself is likely to have picked up his surgical knowledge from the doctor from whom he bought his freedom.

Finally they put in writing what **recompense** each man should have if wounded or maimed on that voyage. So, for the loss of a right arm, 600 pieces of eight or six slaves; for the loss of a left arm, 500 pieces of eight or five slaves; for a right leg, 500 pieces of eight or five slaves; for the left leg, 400 pieces of eight or four slaves; for an eye, 100 pieces of eight or one slave; for a finger the same as for an eye. All is paid from the common stock.

An exact division is made of any left over; the captain gets five or six parts where the ordinary seaman gets one. The mate gets two, and other officers may get more than one. Even the boys on board get a half share. It is forbidden for anyone to take anything from the **prizes** until the final reckoning. They swear not to do this, and if someone breaks this rule, he is turned out. They are kind to each other and will often give something they have to another who wants it. They put their prisoners ashore as soon as possible, keeping a few if they need servants, whom they will release after two or three years.

A mixture of pieces of eight and Spanish and Dutch coins from the time. Pieces of eight were Spanish coins, worth about eight Spanish reals (the real being valued at about 12 1/2 cents). They had the number 8 on them and were accepted as currency all over the Caribbean, not just on the islands controlled by Spain.

CHAPTER 7

Pirate
Tortures

This print is from the 1678 Dutch edition of Exquemelin's book. It shows the pirates after they have captured the town of Puerto de Principe, torturing prisoners to make them say where their treasure was hidden.

The pirates would torture people to make them say where other people were hiding, or where their goods were hidden. They put them to the **rack** and beat them with sticks. Others had burning **matches** placed between their fingers, while others had cords twisted about their heads until their eyes stood out of their heads. Even if they had nothing to confess, they died of these inhuman tortures.

One man was said, falsely, to be rich. When he said he had only 100 pieces of eight, which he had already given to the pirates, they would not believe him and stretched him on the rack, despite his age, until both his arms were broken. They then tied his thumbs and toes with cords and hung him from four stakes, so that his whole weight was held by his thumbs and toes. They laid a great stone on him, as if to press him, and put burning palm leaves in his face, until they had burned his skin, face, and beard almost all off. At last they tied him to a pillar and gave him only enough food to keep him barely alive until he spoke. After five days he said he would try to get some money, as much as 500 pieces of eight. This was a small sum to the pirates, and they demanded more, but at last he convinced them that he was but a poor tavern keeper and could get no more. They let him raise it and let him go, though it would be a miracle if he long survived his release. There were other pirate tortures that this man was not put to. Some were crucified. Others had their feet stuck in a fire and were burned alive. They would do this to white men and their black slaves, with equal cruelty.

PUTTING TORTURE IN PERSPECTIVE

The tortures that the pirates used were appalling. They must, however, be looked at in the context of the time. In the seventeenth century torture was seen as one of the methods that might sensibly be used to force information from people. European governments frequently used torture and mutilation to extract confessions from their prisoners. It was a time when people accused of witchcraft were often burned or hanged, having been tortured to confess. The crime of treason in Britain was punishable by hanging, drawing and quartering (a process of torture after hanging).

BARTHOLOMEUS DE PORTUGEES,

Hooft van een partij Franse
en Engelse Roovers,

CHAPTER 8

Tales of the Early Pirates

The first pirate on Tortuga was Pierre Le Grand. He captured the Vice Admiral of the Spanish fleet with only one boat and 28 men to help him. They attacked out of desperation, for they had seen no prey for a long time. They attacked at dusk. Armed with only a pistol in one hand and a sword in the other, they boarded the ship, reached the captain's cabin, and held the captain and his officers at gunpoint. Then they seized the ammunition stores, and the ship was captured. They set the Spanish ashore and sailed with the treasure back to France. It was this success that set the planters and hunters of Tortuga thinking of piracy as a trade. They set out in canoes, seizing boats and goods around the Cape of Alvarez, where many trading ships passed. The boats they took enabled them to go farther, up the coast to Campeche or even to the mainland.

A pirate called Bartholomew Portuges sailed with 30 men out of Jamaica and met a trading ship, protected by 20 great guns and 70 men. He attacked again and again, refusing to give up, until he finally took the ship. The wind was against a return to Jamaica, so they made for St. Anthony, west of Cuba, to repair themselves and take on water, which they badly needed. But they were sighted by three great ships from Spain, bound for Havana. There was no escape. They were captured, and all of them made prisoners.

The ships docked at Campeche, and the authorities on shore demanded Portuges to **try** on land. The Spanish feared he would escape on shore (as he had done before), so they kept him on board, erecting a **gibbet** to hang him the next day. Portuges heard the gibbet going up and decided to escape. He took two earthenware wine jars to help him swim. He stole the knife from his meal, and when everyone slept, he waited, hoping his sentry would sleep, too. But he did not, and Portuges stabbed him and leaped into the sea. He swam to the shore with the help of the jars, although he had never learned to swim. He hid in the woods, where he could not be found by the people who searched for him. After several days he headed for the coast, arriving a fortnight (two weeks) after his escape from the ship. He crossed several large rivers on a crude raft made from stout twigs. He had nothing but herbs to eat and a little water to drink. Once he reached the coast, he found shellfish on the rocks.

Portuges was lucky to find a pirate ship anchored at the Cape Golfo Trieste, with comrades from Jamaica. He asked them to help him to return to Campeche to recapture the ship he had escaped from. They agreed and equipped him a boat with 20 men. Eight days later they arrived, attacked the ship unawares, and compelled the Spanish to surrender. Being masters of the ship, they weighed anchor and set sail to avoid pursuit.

ROBBING THE SPANISH

Early pirates concentrated their piracy on the Spanish. This was partly chance —most of the ships in the area at the time were Spanish. It was also deliberate. Most of the pirates had left the mainland because of disputes with the Spanish, which was one good reason to make them a target for raids. Also the Spanish ships were more likely to be full of gold and other valuable goods.

Earthenware wine jars of the sort that were used in the Caribbean at this time. It was jars like these that Portuges might have used to escape from the ship he was imprisoned on.

They set sail for Jamaica, but near the island of Pinos, south of Cuba, fortune turned her face against Portuges again. A horrible storm drove the ship against some rocks, and the ship was lost. Portuges and his companions escaped by canoe.

Once he had returned to Jamaica, Portuges soon set about more piracy with fresh men. But what they managed to gain by their wicked deeds, they soon spent on drink, gambling, and women. Portuges was never lucky in any of his ventures, and he continually lost all his fortune. I saw him die in the very extreme of poverty.

As the numbers of pirates grew, the Spanish cut down their shipping and had their ships travel in larger, more defended groups. This did them no good, however, for the pirates, finding fewer ships at sea, formed larger companies and began to attack the towns of **New Spain.**

This made the Spanish losses worse than ever.

The first pirate to try a land invasion was Lewis Scott, who sacked and pillaged Campeche. After him came Edward Mansvelt, who was a pirate around Grenada, but the island of St. Catherine was the first land he took. John Davis ought not to be forgotten, as his were some of the most remarkable pirate deeds. He decided to land in Nicaragua with eighty men, leaving ten to guard his ship. They landed in the port at night, coming in silently by canoe. They traveled inland up the river by canoe at night, hiding in the bushes by day. They arrived at the city on the third night and convinced the sentry that they were Spanish fishermen, being well able to speak the Spanish language. They killed the sentry and entered the city. They robbed as many houses as they could, and churches, too. The alarm was raised, and many citizens banded together to defend the town. The pirates fled, taking all they had stolen with them, and a few prisoners as hostages. They got on board and then saw 500 Spanish troops, well armed, on the shore. They fired on the Spanish and luckily escaped. They stole about 4,000 pieces of eight in ready money. Also they had gold plate and jewels worth about 50,000 pieces of eight, or more. But after a while they had spent it and had to seek more.

John Davis was chosen as Admiral of seven or eight pirate boats as he was agreed to be a good conductor of such enterprises. They began by heading north of Cuba to attack the Spanish fleet, which was due to leave New Spain; but the fleet did not come. Then the pirates made for the coast of Florida and sacked the city of St. Augustine, which had a garrison of some 200 men. These could not prevent the **pillage** of the city; the pirates were not harmed by either soldiers or townsmen.

The early pirates were able to take advantage of the unexpectedness of their attacks to raid other ships at sea. Once piracy was known to be going on in the Caribbean, ships were more cautious and traveled in larger groups. Spanish ships would often travel with warships. This made them more difficult targets, and it was this practice that first drove the pirates to attack ports and even inland towns. Towns were also more predictable targets. Pirates might guess where ships would pass, but they could not be sure of the time or the place.

Henry Morgan was the son of a wealthy Welsh farmer. He went to Barbados in the service of one who, as is commonly done, sold him as soon as they landed. He served his time and then went to Jamaica to seek new fortunes. He joined some pirates and after several profitable voyages agreed with some of his comrades to jointly buy a ship. They chose him **unanimously** as their captain. They cruised the shores of Campeche and took several ships. On Morgan's return he found another pirate, Edward Mansvelt, busy equipping a large fleet of ships to land on the mainland and pillage whatever came his way. Mansvelt, seeing Morgan's prizes, and judging him to be courageous, chose him as Vice Admiral for the expedition. They captured the islands of St. Catherine, which Mansvelt decided to try to keep. He returned to Jamaica for men to fortify the islands, but the Governor of Jamaica did not like to weaken his forces. Mansvelt decided to try the Governor of Tortuga, but died on the way there. The Spanish recaptured the islands.

Morgan made new plans. He equipped a ship and ordered his fleet to meet at a Cuban port, where he would call a Council to decide where to attack. After two months he had a fleet of 12 sail, with 700 fighting men, English and French. At the Council some thought it would be best to attack the city of Havana, in Cuba, under cover of darkness. Others suggested other attempts. The first proposal was rejected, as many of the pirates had been prisoners in Havana. They said it would need at least 1,500 men to succeed, and that they saw no possibility of gathering so great a fleet. So it was decided to attack another place. At last someone suggested the town of Puerto de Principe, saying he knew it well. Because it was inland, it had never been sacked by pirates, and its inhabitants were rich from trade. Morgan and his chief officers agreed to this. They set sail, steering for the coast nearest Puerto de Principe. That night a Spanish prisoner swam ashore and told the townspeople the pirates' plot, which he had overheard. The Spanish began to hide their riches and to carry away what they could. The Governor raised the townsmen, both freedmen and slaves. He ordered some to cut down trees and lay them across the path, to hinder progress. He placed several **ambushes**, with cannon to fire on the invading pirates. The rest were left in the town, where they could see the pirates coming from a long way off. The govenor had, in all, about 800 men.

Morgan and his men found the paths so impenetrable that they took to the woods, thereby escaping the ambushes, and reached the open ground around the town. The Governor sent a troop of horsemen to charge the pirates, thinking to break them up, put them to flight, and chase them away. But the pirates marched in good order, to their drum, with flying colors, and attacked the Spanish.

Henry Morgan as a young man, painted before he set out for the West Indies.

CHAPTER 9

The Early Career of Henry Morgan

PIRATES AND PRIVATEERS

It may seem surprising that pirates such as Edward Mansvelt would turn to the governors of various islands, no matter which country they were claimed by, for help in pirate raids. They could do this because there was, at the time, a very thin line between piracy—robbery at sea— and privateering— robbery at sea on behalf of a particular country. Pirates who attacked the Spanish with the support of the English or French governors (the official representatives of their home countries) were acting "officially." For much of Henry Morgan's career as a pirate, he would return to Jamaica and report to the Governor there, Sir Thomas Modyford, who would regularly protest that Morgan had done more than he was supposed to. Yet he always gave Morgan another commission.

25

Pirate raids on towns followed a set pattern, based on early experiences. The pirates liked to make a stealthy approach to the town, in the hope of taking people by surprise. Not only did this mean there would be less resistance, it also meant that people had less time to hide their valuables. Once the town was taken, the pirates tried to round up all the prisoners and valuables that they could as quickly as possible. The longer they spent in the town the more likely it was that word of their attack would get to the Spanish army, who would come to relieve the town. As soon as they felt they had enough treasure, they would demand ransoms for both individual prisoners and the town itself. At this point they were often in a hurry to go and settled for much less than at first they had demanded.

The Spanish fought bravely, but seeing the pirates were skilled fighters, and that the Governor and many of the soldiers were killed, they began to retreat to the wood for safety; but most were killed before they reached it. The pirates entered the town, despite great resistance from those inside. Many people, seeing the enemy in the town, shut themselves up in their houses and fired at the pirates, who threatened them, saying, "Surrender, or you shall soon see the town in flames, and your wives and children torn to pieces before your faces." So the Spanish gave in, fearing eventually to be beaten. The pirates shut up the Spanish and their slaves and gathered all the goods they could find. Then they searched the countryside around the town, finding more goods, prisoners, and provisions. So they fell to feasting, but did not feed the poor prisoners. They tormented the prisoners daily to make them confess where their goods were hidden. They even refused food to the women and children; most of them died. When they could find no more to rob, and provisions became scarce, the pirates decided to seek new fortunes in other places. They told the prisoners to find money to ransom themselves, or they would all be taken to Jamaica and sold. They also had to ransom the town, or every house would be reduced to ashes.

The Spanish chose four people to go and seek the ransoms. After some days they returned, saying, "We have searched everywhere, and yet we have found no one, so we have nothing. But if you will be patient, we will find what you demand within fifteen days." Captain Morgan agreed. Soon after, some pirates who had been searching the woods and fields returned with considerable booty, and a Negro carrying letters from the Governor of Santiago to the prisoners, saying, "Do not hurry to pay any ransoms; put off the pirates with excuses and delays. In a short while I will come to your aid." When Morgan was told, he had all the booty carried on to the ships and told the Spanish to pay their ransoms the very next day, or he would burn the town. He did not tell them about the letter. They tried to delay him. Morgan, knowing why, decided to leave. He demanded 500 cattle, and salt to salt them, and went back to his ship, with six prisoners as a pledge for what he had demanded. The next day the Spanish brought the cattle and salt. Morgan refused to return the prisoners until they had helped to butcher and salt the meat. This done, he set the prisoners free.

Meanwhile the English and French pirates fell out. An Englishman took one of the marrow bones of an ox that a Frenchman was butchering. They decided on a **duel.** But the Englishman stabbed the Frenchman in the back, before he could defend himself. The French rose against the English for this. Captain Morgan stepped in, commanding that the Englishman be chained and taken to Jamaica, where justice would be done. (It was done; he was hanged.)

As soon as all was ready, they sailed to an island to divide their booty. They found they had only 50,000 pieces of eight, which would not even pay their debts in Jamaica. So Morgan suggested another raid before going home. The French decided to go home, leaving the English alone.

This engraving shows Morgan's attack on Puerto de Principe, and is taken from an edition of Exquemelin's book. The attackers and defenders are similarly armed. This is not too surprising; most of the pirates' weapons were captured on raids like this.

The Capture of Puerto Bello

Captain Morgan convinced his men that even without the French they could get riches. He had nine ships and 460 men. He kept his plan secret, saying only that with luck they would have a successful voyage. They sailed toward the mainland, soon reaching the coast of Costa Rica. As soon as they sighted land, Morgan told them they were to plunder Puerto Bello by night and sack the city. He had told them at the last minute, so no one could warn the town of their coming. Some feared they had not enough men to attack so great a city. Morgan replied, "If our numbers are small, our hearts are great. And the fewer we are, the better share in the spoils we shall have."

The city has two strong **castles** at the entry to the port to defend it and a garrison of 300 soldiers. The merchants do not live here, because the air is unhealthy. But there are large warehouses, where they bring plate and the rest from Panama on mules, and where the slave ships come to sell slaves. They landed west of Puerto Bello and followed the river inland as far as their ships could go. They left a few men to guard the fleet and took to canoes. About midnight they landed and marched on the city, guided by an Englishman who had been a prisoner there. He and four others were sent to capture the sentry. They were so cunning that he had no time to cry out, or fire a warning from his musket. They took him to Captain Morgan, who asked many questions about the city and its defenses, threatening that he would have the truth or kill him. They moved toward the city, taking the sentry with them.

At last they reached and surrounded the first castle. Morgan told the sentry to tell the **garrison** to surrender, or they would be cut into pieces, with no mercy shown to anyone. They did not listen to these threats, firing at the pirates instead, which warned the city. But despite a great resistance, the soldiers of the castle had to surrender to the pirates. The pirates decided to keep their word, to strike terror in the rest of the city. They blew up the whole castle, with the Spanish inside. Then they attacked the city, which had not yet organized its defense. People hid their money and jewels in wells or in **cisterns**, or buried it. The Governor could not organize the citizens, so he withdrew to the remaining castle with his men. The pirates attacked vigorously.

The assault lasted from daybreak until noon, when it was still not clear who would win. At last the pirates, seeing that they had heavy losses and little gain, thought of using **fireballs** to burn the doors of the castle. But as they drew close, the Spanish dropped great quantities of stones and pots of gunpowder, which forced them to retreat. Morgan began to despair and could hardly think what to do. Just then he saw the English colors raised at a smaller fort that his men were attacking, and was sent word of their victory. This gave him fresh courage, and he decided to make a fresh assault on the main castle, where most of

SIEGES

A town that had forts, or at least a garrison of soldiers, was usually more difficult for the pirates to capture, but it was likely to have far more worth stealing. Sieges were similar to the raids on towns, except the pirates needed to be more heavily armed. They seem to have obeyed on the whole general rules for conducting sieges that applied in wars at the time: they usually offered a surrender at the start, and then again when they were sure to win. If surrender was made, it was common to be merciful and spare people's lives. If there was no surrender until the town was entered, the winners were likely to be far less merciful to those inside the town.

A glass hand grenade, found on the wreck of a pirate ship that sank off Tortuga some time in the 1670s. Glass was seen as a good container for explosives, because when the grenade went off, the slivers of glass that flew out were as lethal as the explosion itself. Many pirates did not have the luxury of such grenades. They had to improvise, using gunpowder to fill whatever containers they could find.

the rich citizens had fled for protection. He had ten or twelve wide ladders made and ordered some captured monks and nuns to stand the ladders against the walls of the castle, certain that the Governor would not shoot at them. But he was mistaken. The Governor did his duty, although the monks and nuns begged him to give up the castle and spare his and their own lives. Nearly all of them were killed before they finally fixed the ladders. The pirates mounted the ladders quickly and threw fireballs among the Spanish. They were so fierce that the Spanish could no longer defend the castle, threw down their arms, and pleaded for mercy. Only the Governor continued to kill pirates, and the soldiers who would not stand. The pirates offered him **quarter**, but he replied, "I would rather die a brave soldier than be hanged a coward!" They tried to take him prisoner, but he resisted so fiercely that they were forced to kill him. It was night by the time the pirates took the castle, so they shut up the prisoners and feasted in their usual manner, that is to say, to excess.

The next day they questioned the prisoners about where their riches were hidden. Because they got no answers, they tortured them so cruelly that many died. None were spared except for those who told the pirates where their treasure was hidden. The pirates stayed in the port for some two weeks, at the end of which disease was raging in the city. Much sickness was due to the foulness of the air from all the unburied corpses, for the pirates had not buried any of them. Most of the pirates' own wounded died, and many fell sick. They decided that it was time to leave the city.

Word of the attack reached the President of Panama, and he set about raising a force to eject the pirates. But their ships were nearby, and they intended to seize what they could, set the city on fire, and leave. So they carried their pillage on board, provisioning the ship for the voyage. Meanwhile Morgan told the prisoners to pay a ransom or their city would be reduced to ashes. He sent two prisoners to raise 100,000 pieces of eight. They went to the President of Panama, who made for Puerto Bello, to catch the pirates before they sailed. The pirates did not flee, but ambushed the force at a narrow pass and put most of the Spanish to flight. The President was obliged to withdraw. He sent a

A diver bringing up a cutlass from the same pirate shipwreck as the hand grenade on page 29.

message to Morgan saying, "If you do not leave Puerto Bello at once, you can expect no quarter when I take the city, as I shall soon do." Morgan, knowing his ships were on hand for a quick departure, replied, "I will not hand over the castles without the money I demanded. If it is not paid, I will burn the whole city, demolishing the castles and killing the prisoners."

The President saw that the pirates could not be brought to reason. He decided to leave them to come to terms with the citizens as best they might. He was astounded that they could have captured so great and well-defended a city with only 400 men and without the use of cannon. He sent a messenger to Morgan, asking that he might be allowed to see the marvelous weapons that had allowed them to have so great a victory. Morgan was polite to the messenger and gave him an old pistol and some thirty bullets to fire from it. He begged him to present the weapons with which the port had been captured to the President and to tell him that they were only a loan, and that in a year or so he would come to Panama himself to collect them.

The messenger returned with thanks for the pistol, and also a ring for Morgan as a gift, made of gold and inset with rubies and diamonds. He said the President had told him to tell Captain Morgan that he should not trouble himself to come to Panama to collect the pistol. He also said that if Morgan were to visit Panama in the way that he had visited Puerto Bello, he would have a different, and less profitable, reception.

The miserable citizens raised 100,000 pieces of eight. The pirates sailed for Cuba, found a quiet spot, and divided up the spoils. They had 250,000 pieces of eight, besides linen, silks, and other valuables. They sailed home to Jamaica and spent the dividends they had gained with so much toil in the usual way.

UNDERWATER ARCHAEOLOGY

Underwater archaeology is much more than finding wrecks and bringing up all the things that can be found on them. It is as careful as land archaeology. Areas marked off with tape are excavated slowly and carefully, layer by layer. Drawings are made of each stage of the process to record exactly where things have been found. Archaeologists have had to work out techniques for excavating underwater and keeping records of those excavations. Raising heavy objects also causes problems, as do cleaning and preserving them once they are exposed to air. Careful excavations of this type can tell us a lot about the way that people lived on board ship, and maybe even how the ship sank.

CHAPTER 11

Sailing with Morgan to Panama

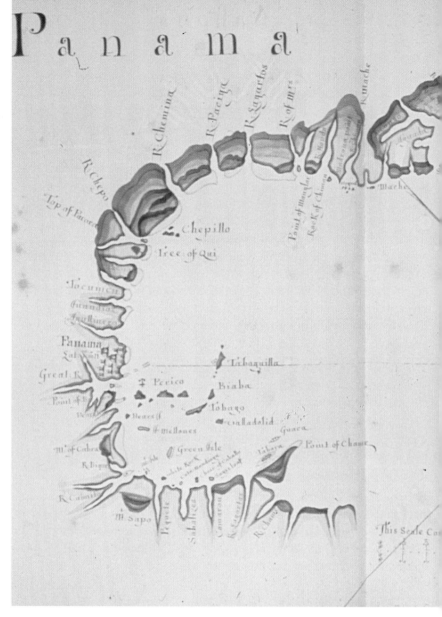

This map shows the Caribbean around the area of Panama, and the places that Morgan visited.

Morgan was now famous for his exploits. He successfully attacked the mainland again, around Maracaibo. Then he decided the time was right to attack Panama itself. Huge numbers joined him, with ships and canoes; some even walked. My ship was among them. On October 24, 1670, Morgan called a Council to discuss provisioning so many people. They sent five ships to the mainland to get corn by raiding the towns and villages. Others hunted in the woods for cattle and pigs to be salted down. Others made the ships ready for sea.

The ships sent for corn were becalmed in sight of the coast for several days. But though they could not reach the villages, they did attack a ship loaded with corn and captured it. The next day the wind changed.

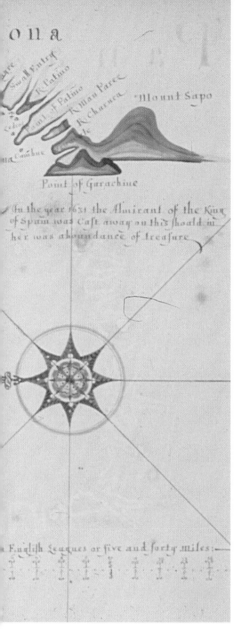

They landed and met with fierce opposition. In the end the Spanish fled to the woods. The pirates chased them and tortured those they caught to make them show where their goods were hidden. After fifteen days they had prisoners, plate, and valuables and decided to return, first demanding a ransom for the town of 4,000 **bushels** of corn. Morgan had almost given them up; they had been gone some five weeks. The corn and salted meat were divided, and they set sail and were joined by more ships. So they now had 37 ships, 2,000 fighting men, and also mariners and boys. Morgan's ship had 28 guns. They had a great deal of ammunition. Morgan divided the ships into two squadrons. They then agreed on the division of the spoils. Besides the usual shares, anyone distinguished in battle would get 50 pieces of eight. The first ship to take a Spanish ship would get a tenth of the cargo. They then debated between Cartagena, Panama, or Santa Cruz; Panama was chosen. But first it was decided to retake the island of St. Catherine.

They weighed anchor on December 16. Four days later they reached St. Catherine. Morgan took 1,000 men ashore. They were opposed by the Spanish and could not advance. They had to wait out of range all day, with nothing to eat. About midnight it began to rain hard. Most of the pirates wore only a pair of breeches and a shirt, with neither shoes nor stockings. They pulled down some deserted houses to make fires, and the next day they set off again. But it rained again, even harder; they could not attack.

PANAMA

Most of the silver the Spanish mined and sent to Spain was stored in Panama. The silver was brought there either on muleback, overland, or up the Chagres River. Because of the silver, Panama was heavily defended. This led to its being used as a huge warehouse for all sorts of goods, including slaves. Until Morgan's attack, there had never been a successful raid on Panama.

AMBUSCADES

As Morgan and his men made their way to Panama, they were continually coming across what Exquemelin calls ambuscades. These were more than just ambushes. Groups of soldiers would spy on the pirates and send word back about their progress. They also hoped to catch one or two stragglers, or to find the opportunity to kill some of the pirates. The soldiers were not meant to attack if they were clearly outnumbered. This explains why they never actually stayed to fight.

They were now very miserable and hungry. They found a scabby old horse, which they killed, roasted, and ate without salt or bread, more like wolves than men. Morgan heard the men grumbling and saw they would soon want to return to the ships. He demanded that the Spanish surrender or be put to the sword without mercy. The Governor said he could not hold out against Morgan's fleet, so he would surrender. He asked Morgan to help him save his reputation by attacking from land and sea that night, all firing bullets into the air. This was agreed to, and that night the false battle began and the island was taken. Morgan asked if there were any who knew Panama and found three who said they did. He offered them a share of the loot to come as guides, and they accepted.

So Morgan sent five ships and some men to take the castle of Chagre, which guarded the river up to Panama. Captain Brodley led the attack on Chagre (he had sailed with Morgan and Mansvelt). The fighting was fierce, but the castle was taken. One of the prisoners said the Governor of Panama had been warned of the pirates' intentions, and that he had strengthened his garrison from 150 to 314 men, all well armed. There were also ambuscades along the river, and 3,600 soldiers camping in the open fields waiting for the pirates. When Morgan heard Chagre was taken, he went there at once. At Chagre, he made the prisoners build new walls for the castle and took all Spanish boats on the river. Leaving a garrison at Chagre, and guards on the captured ships, they set sail for Panama.

They had few provisions, intending to rob small towns along the way. They left on August 18, 1670—five boats with artillery, thirty-two canoes, and 1,200 men. On the first day they reached the town of Bracos, where they rested and stretched their limbs from the cramped conditions of the boats. They searched for provisions but could find none; the Spanish had all fled. So most had only a pipe of tobacco at the end of their first day. At the beginning of the third day, the river had become very shallow. They tried walking, but it proved to be impossible. They returned to the boats and with great difficulty went up the river as far as Cadro Buena. They were now desperate with hunger.

On the fourth day one guide scouted ahead, looking for ambuscades. The second guide followed with the canoes, making very slow progress. The third led a land party. At about noon they heard of an ambuscade, which they hoped meant they could capture some food. But the Spanish had fled, leaving nothing but a small number of leather bags (all empty), and a few crumbs on the ground. The pirates fell to eating the leather bags, wanting anything to fill their stomachs. So they made a banquet of the bags of leather, even quarrelling over how they were to be shared. So great was their hunger that had they met any Spanish, they would have roasted or boiled them at once.

A French picture of a buccaneer and his dogs. Buccaneers were said to be exceptionally accurate shots, because of the practice they got while hunting. The leather bags that the pirates ate would have been about this size.

After eating the leather, they set out again and reached another port. Another ambuscade had been laid and deserted, as before. They still could not find anything to eat. Those who had saved some leather from their noon feast made it supper. You may ask how the pirates could eat leather. I only answer that if you were in the same extremity, you would have done just as the pirates did. They sliced the leather into strips and beat it between two stones, and wet it and beat it again. Then they scraped off the hair and roasted or boiled it on a fire. When it was cooked, they cut it into small scraps and washed it down with frequent gulps of water, which was to hand.

A collection of cannon found in the same pirate wreck as the glass grenade (page 29) and the cutlass (page 30). These cannon came from France, Holland, Portugal, and Spain. The range of countries shows that the pirates were prepared to attack ships of any country at this time, and that they took anything that was useful, not just gold.

On the fifth day at about noon, the pirates came to Barbacoa, which was left as before. There were several plantations nearby, but there was no food there either. Finally they found in a small cave two sacks of meal and wheat, two great jars of wine, and some fruit called **plantains.** Captain Morgan, seeing they were all nearly dead of hunger, made a careful division of the food, giving a little more to the weakest. Then they marched on. Those too weak to walk were taken by canoe. That night they rested at a plantation, which was as bare as all before.

On the sixth day they marched on, but they were getting slower. They were even eating raw herbs and grass. Then at noon they found a plantation where a barrel full of corn had been left, which they divided up and ate. An hour or so more on their journey, they found an Indian ambuscade point, but no provisions. There were about 100

Indians on the opposite bank of the river. Some pirates leaped into the river, hoping to give chase, but in vain. The Indians were much more nimble on their feet and even managed to shoot at the pirates from the trees.

They found that they needed to cross the river to continue their march on the other side. They slept, but not well, and there were murmurings against Captain Morgan and desirings to return home. There were others who would rather die than go back with nothing, and others who tried to encourage their companions, saying that they would soon meet with better fortunes.

On the morning of the seventh day, they cleaned their weapons and crossed the river, arriving around noon at the village of Cruz. They could see smoke from the chimneys and were greatly cheered, thinking that smoke meant people and food. They hurried into the town, only to be disappointed yet again; the smoke was not from cooking fires. The Spanish had, before leaving the village, set fire to their own houses; and had left no beasts behind. The pirates did come across a few unlucky stray cats and dogs, which they immediately cooked and ate. Then in the King's stable (which none had dared to burn), they found fifteen or sixteen jars of wine and a huge sack of bread. They began to eat and drink, but all fell sick at once. They feared poison, but really the sickness was just the result of food on top of long hunger. They were so sick that they had to stay there until the next day.

They were now twenty-six leagues from Chagre and eight from Panama, and the boats and canoes could absolutely go no farther. Captain Morgan had to land all his men, no matter how weak they were. One canoe was hidden, to be used by spies. The rest were returned to where they had left the boats. The Spanish were thought to have fled the village to nearby plantations, so Morgan said no one was to leave the village in case of attack. One party did slip out looking for food, but it was attacked by both Spanish and Indians and had a man taken prisoner.

On the eighth day, Morgan sent an advance guard to find the best way to Panama and to check if there were any places where an ambuscade could be laid. After ten hours of marching these men

SCORCHED EARTH
The strategy that the Spanish used against the pirates was a very common one, much in use in wars of the time, called a "scorched earth" policy. It was used by the inhabitants of a place against invaders, especially if they had some idea of where the invaders were heading. The inhabitants would destroy their own homes and supplies ahead of advancing invaders, in the hope of starving them before they reached their destination, or at least weakening them so much that they could be easily beaten.

were fired on by some 3,000–4,000 arrows, which seemed after long examination to come from caves high in the rocky pass. At last the firing stopped, and the pirates went on into the forest. They spotted some Indians running on, while others stopped to fight. This they did bravely, until their leader was killed. The rest escaped. They were too swift for the pirates to take any prisoners. There were eight pirates dead and ten wounded.

The pirates reached open ground and could see some Indians, standing close to where they must pass. Fifty men went to take some prisoners, but the Indians were too nimble. There were high hills on either side of the open ground. The Indians took one hill, the pirates the other. Morgan had come up and was sure there was an ambuscade point in the wood. He sent men to search. But the Indians came off the hill and melted away into the woods, to be seen no more. That night it rained heavily. The pirates looked for shelter but found only a few small huts, which could keep their weapons dry. There was no food. A few men stayed in the huts to guard the weapons; the rest were out in the rain all night. The ninth day dawned dry, but the ground was slippery and difficult. After two hours they saw about twenty Spanish watching them but could not catch any, because they hid in secret caves among the rocks.

At last at the top of a mountain, they saw the South Sea (Pacific Ocean) below them and were as happy as if this was all they had wanted to accomplish. They could see ships sailing from Panama toward Tobago. As they came down the mountain, they found hidden in a valley a herd of cattle, which they killed. While some butchered the cattle, others got wood to kindle fires to roast them. They threw chunks of meat onto the fire and ate them while they were half roasted, because of their hunger. They looked like cannibals at this feast, their beards and chests all red with blood. Having eaten, they marched on. Morgan sent fifty men ahead to see if they could get some prisoners. They saw about twenty Spanish in the distance but could not get close. Shortly after, they sighted the highest steeple of Panama and jumped for joy and threw their hats into the air, laughing and shouting as if Panama was already taken.

They pitched camp, impatient to attack the city in the morning. The Spanish heard the cheering and came out of the city to check on the pirates, keeping well out of range. They called that they would all meet in the morning and returned to the city, leaving eight or nine horsemen to watch the pirates. The pirates, meanwhile, posted sentries and ate their meal with every sign of content, and then slept. Early on the tenth morning, they marched on the city. Because Morgan thought they might be ambushed on the road, they took the more difficult route

NATIVE INDIANS

The Spanish had been settling South America for nearly 200 years by 1670, the date of Morgan's raid on Panama. Their attitude to the native peoples of America was consistent throughout this time. They saw the Indians as savages. The first Spanish troops saw no need to live peacefully, on equal terms—the Indians were robbed of their land and valuables, and then either killed or used as servants. But by 1670 the Spanish controlled so much land that their troops were spread thinly. Most of their troops protected vital ports, such as Panama. Indians who lived without disturbing the Spanish were allowed to go their own way.

through the woods. When the Spanish realized they must be coming a way that they had not defended, they had to come out to meet them. The force consisted of the Governor of Panama, two squadrons, four regiments of foot, and many wild bulls, herded by slaves and Indians. The pirates saw the city below and the Spanish coming to meet them. They divided into troops, sending 200 buccaneers ahead—the best shots of the party. The Spanish had waited on open ground and charged when they saw the pirates. But the ground was boggy, and their horses stuck and could not maneuver. The buccaneers started shooting. The

A print of a buccaneer from an edition of Exquemelin's book. The buccaneers were pirates who had originally been hunters. They were by far the best shots, so during a raid they were often sent ahead as snipers.

The battle for Panama, as drawn for the Dutch edition of Exquemelin's book. As the picture was not drawn in Panama at the time of the battle, but was drawn especially to illustrate Exquemelin's story, it does not prove that his account is accurate.

Spanish tried to stampede the bulls at the pirates, but most of the cattle ran away, frightened by the noise of battle. The battle went on for two hours, at the end of which the Spanish horsemen were ruined and the rest fled. The pirates were too exhausted to follow, but they searched the dunes by the shore for stragglers, whom they killed. They found a captain who told them the size of the army. He also told where trenches had been dug and guns placed.

Morgan reviewed his men and found more wounded and killed than he had thought, although they had killed over 600 Spanish. The pirates marched on the city, although the approach was difficult. The Spanish fired their cannon incessantly at the pirates; many were killed. Yet they still advanced, and at the end of three hours, they had reached the city. The Spanish were forced to surrender. The pirates entered the city and killed as many as they could. The inhabitants had hidden their goods, but there were many warehouses full of silks and cloth and linen and other things. Captain Morgan gathered his men together and commanded none should drink wine, saying it was all poisoned by the Spanish. The real reason was that he wanted them sober for the days ahead. He placed guards on the city and captured a ship that was stuck in the mud and unable to flee. Then secretly he ordered that the city be set on fire; no one knows why he did this. Soon the whole city was ablaze.

Defe acthete fien op fol: 131

Morgan convinced his men and the citizens that it was done by the Spanish. His men tried to put it out, by blowing up and pulling down houses to stop its progress. But most of the houses in the city were built of wood and soon burned. Much of value was destroyed, including a great number of slaves who were hiding in the warehouses.

Most of the pirates camped outside the city, waiting for another Spanish attack. Men went to Chagre with news of the victory. The Spanish appeared from time to time, but lacked the courage to attack. Morgan and some men reentered the city, looking for lodgings, which were hard to find in the wreckage, and looking for valuables that had survived the fire. Many riches were found, especially in the wells and cisterns, hidden for safety. The next day Morgan took men to seek the inhabitants of Panama who had fled. After two days they returned with over 200 prisoners. Morgan sent the captured boat, now clear of the mud, into the South Sea. It came back with three boats that it had captured, and the news of a galleon loaded with treasure. They had captured it, but it slipped away as they were feasting to celebrate its capture. When Morgan heard this, he sent all of his ships to find the galleon, but in vain. They returned to the island of Tobago, where they found and took two ships with about 20,000 pieces of eight. They then returned to Panama.

MORGAN SUES THE PRINTERS

The Spanish were outraged at Morgan's attack on Panama. He was captured and sent back to England. He was later sent back to the Caribbean in 1675 as Deputy Governor of Jamaica! Morgan said that he had been acting as a privateer, and not for personal gain. He tried hard to play down stories of his cruelty and of his hidden wealth. He was furious with his image as a cruel and violent man in Exquemelin's account of the sack of Panama. When the English editions of Exquemelin's book came out in 1684, he sued the printers for libel. He demanded £10,000 from each of them. He was only awarded £200 from each, but they had to promise to produce new editions that did not discuss Morgan's cruelties in such detail.

WHAT HAPPENED TO HENRY MORGAN?

Morgan returned to Jamaica, where he was thanked by the Governor for his work in attacking Panama. When Morgan had set out with a commission to attack Spanish ports and destroy all the Spanish stores he could find, the Governor had thought that England and Spain would soon be at war. But unknown to him, a treaty had been signed between the English and Spanish in Madrid. The Governor was summoned to England to answer charges of encouraging the pirates against the Spanish. In 1672, Morgan was arrested and sent back to England to face charges of piracy. However, by November 1674 he was so much in the King's favor that he was knighted and sent back to Jamaica as Deputy Governor. He remained in Jamaica, a rich and powerful man. He never actually became Governor, but acted as such in the interval between one Governor leaving and being replaced with another. He died in 1688.

The men Morgan sent to Chagre returned with news that the pirates of Chagre had captured a Spanish ship, which they had lured into the port by flying Spanish colors and chasing the ship with a pirate ship. The Spanish ship fled to "safety," only to find itself snared and seized. Morgan decided to stay longer in Panama than he had first intended, for the pirates at Chagre were taking treasure, and those searching the countryside around Panama were finding many prisoners and great riches. The prisoners were tortured to confess where even more treasure was hidden. After three weeks in Panama, Morgan gave orders to prepare to depart. Animals were found to carry the treasure to the ships. Then men were sent to demand a ransom for the town and the prisoners, while others nailed up the great guns of the town.

On February 24, 1671, Morgan left the city of Panama, or rather the place where the city had stood. He took 175 boats full of riches and about 600 prisoners. They arrived at Cruz, and Morgan told the prisoners they had three days to raise their ransom, or they would be sold as slaves. While he waited, he ordered that rice and corn should be found to provision the ships. Many prisoners were ransomed, but not all. Morgan sailed down the river with all the treasure that his ships could carry, some new prisoners from Cruz, and those not ransomed. About halfway to Chagre, Morgan called the pirates together and made them swear that all the treasure was there to be divided up. Then having some experience of these men, he ordered that a search be made for any hidden treasure, yet little was found.

They embarked for Chagre, arriving on March 9. From Chagre, Morgan sent a great boat to Puerto Bello to demand a ransom for the castle of Chagre, which he would otherwise destroy. The reply came that he might do as he pleased; there was no ransom. So the spoil was carefully divided up, with every man getting what had been agreed. Yet many said that not all of the treasure had been divided and told Morgan to his face that he had reserved the best jewels for himself. They felt 200 pieces of eight each was not a fair share of all they had taken. But Morgan was deaf to all complaints, having decided to keep as much as he could.

At last, finding that the pirates hated him, he commanded that the castle should be destroyed and set sail without calling a Council or giving any notice of his departure. Three or four ships went with him, who, the French believe, went shares with Morgan for the greatest part of the spoil. The French would have revenged themselves upon him, had they been able, but it was as much as they could do to find enough provisions to return to Jamaica; Morgan had taken almost everything with him.

A gold plate recovered from the wreck of the Atocha, *a Spanish galleon that sank off the coast of Florida in 1622. Spanish ships carrying treasure were not always sunk by pirates. Bad weather, such as hurricanes, often blew them onto reefs or tipped them into the sea.*

CHAPTER 12

Going Home

Morgan left us in a miserable condition, and we separated to find our own ways home. My party sailed along the coast of Costa Rica, intending to buy provisions and **careen** our ship, for it was unfit to sail home. Soon we reached Boca del Toro, where there are often turtles to eat. Around this port are little islands, with several different groups of Indians who war on each other and the Spanish. Some to the east of the port trade with pirates, but the pirates stole many as slaves. We sailed west and met three of our old company, who had failed to find provisions, Morgan and his people having robbed all. So we steered farther west and here found many turtles. Next we needed water. There was plenty on the islands, but we dared not land at first, because of the trouble between the pirates and Indians before. But we needed water and had to land. We got our water but were attacked. We killed two of the Indians, then set sail, fearing they might return in larger numbers and tear us all into pieces.

We headed for Cape Gracias á Dios, hoping to find provisions, as there were Indians there who still traded with pirates. And this we found. Many Indians here can speak English and French. After we had provisioned ourselves and set the ship as right as we could, we sailed to the island of Pinos. We arrived fifteen days later and had to repair our ship again, for it was still very leaky. Some careened the ship, some went fishing, with four Indians to help. We went hunting with these Indians and killed and salted plenty of beef and turtles. We feasted plentifully and had no fear of attack; all we had to fear were the crocodiles on the island, for they will attack a man when hungry, as one of us discovered. This man and his black slave accidentally fell into a place where a crocodile had hidden her eggs. The animal, with incredible agility, assaulted the pirate and threw him to the ground. He bravely drew his knife and wrestled with the crocodile for some time, and at last killed it. The black slave found him passed out and brought him back to us, and we put him back on the ship. After this the men did not go alone into the woods.

At last we set sail for Jamaica. We found Captain Morgan had already arrived, but none of the others that he had left behind. Morgan was trying to gather men to garrison on St. Catherine but was prevented by the arrival of an English man-of-war, which set all the pirates on their ears. It carried orders that the Governor of Jamaica should return to England to answer charges that he had helped pirates against the Spanish. A new Governor closed the ports to the pirates and said that pirates would not be welcome, nor anyone who attacked the Spanish. Indeed, he had some of them hanged. The pirates did not dare return to Jamaica but joined the French pirates on the island of Tortuga.

NATIVE CUSTOMS

Exquemelin described the customs of the Indians he lived with in some detail. Their burial customs were of especial interest to him. If a husband died before his wife, she had to visit his grave every day for a year with food (the Indians' year lasted fifteen months). At the end of the year, she had to dig him up and clean his bones, and carry them in a rucksack on her back for another whole year. At the end of this time, she hung the bag up by her door to show that she was free to marry again. Exquemelin dryly remarked: "There was no such ceremony for a man to undergo should his wife die first."

An edible turtle, painted by John White in 1585. It is similar to those the pirates would have eaten. Their favorite method of catching the turtles was during the egg-laying season, when they could be caught on land. If it was not the right season, they caught them in shallow water and dragged them onto land. The turtles were slow on land and completely helpless if turned upside down. The Indians hunted them with stone-tipped spears, and were envied by the pirates for their skill at this.

Glossary

ambuscade a sort of ambush, where watching the movement of the enemy was more important than the actual attack.

ambush a group of soldiers lying in wait in a concealed place to attack the enemy.

articles a list of things agreed upon, a type of contract.

barber surgeons barbers who also performed surgery and dentistry, often without any training.

boucans the fires over which early hunters on Hispaniola and Tortuga dried their meat.

buccaneers an early name for pirates, taken from the French word *boucaniers*, the name for the early hunters on Hispaniola and Tortuga.

bushel 4 pecks (about 25 liters).

careen to turn a ship over onto one side to clean and mend the bottom.

castle fort.

cistern a large water storage tank.

credit allowing someone to have goods on a promise to pay, rather than for instant payment.

Cul de Sac the southern and most inhabited area of Tortuga.

Customs of the Coast the rules that the pirates laid down among themselves, and obeyed instead of the laws of any country.

drudgery hard work.

duel a formal fight between two people, fought according to a set of rules. The rules can vary but have to be decided before the fight begins. Duels were usually about some sort of insult or personal quarrel.

dug-out canoe a canoe made from a tree log, hollowed out by starting a fire on one side, relighting it, and digging out the burned wood until the log is hollow enough to sit in.

eight pounder a description of a cannon based on the weight of the cannonball it used.

embark to go on board ship.

factor a representative of a person or company who has the power to act as if he or she were that person or company.

fair a place where animals are bought and sold (at this time there were horse fairs, geese fairs, and so on).

favorable winds winds that are blowing in the direction you want to go; without them ships were often unable to move, or were blown wildly off course.

fireball a ball filled with gunpowder, fixed to explode after it is thrown.

fresh water water for voyages, stored in barrels. It quickly became stale and then vile tasting. Ships stopped as often as they could to replace their water stocks.

garrison soldiers who live in a fort, castle, or town so as to defend it.

gibbet the temporary wooden framework to hang people on.

hide animal skin that has been stripped of flesh and treated to become less stiff.

hog-yards large areas where pigs were shut up at night to keep them safe from wild animals and thieves. They were usually guarded.

indentured servants people who signed a contract with a person or company to work for them for a number of years, after which they would be free. In return they were transported free to another country and given food and clothing.

manioc   also called cassava. A root vegetable, like the potato. There are two kinds: sweet, which can be eaten raw, and bitter, which has to be heated to get rid of the poisonous juice it contains. Manioc was mostly used to make flour, although it could also be eaten as a vegetable.

match   a long cord that was a slow-burning fuse used to light the gunpowder in muskets.

musket   a gun with a longer muzzle than a pistol, an early kind of rifle.

New Spain   the way that South America was often described at the time, since the Pope had given most of South America to the Spanish in 1494.

piece of eight   a Spanish coin, worth 8 reales (the real being valued at about 12 1/2 cents), which was marked with the number 8. These coins were used as money throughout the Caribbean, not just in Spanish-controlled areas.

pillage   uncontrolled robbery with violence.

pirate   someone who robs another for personal gain, at sea, or from ships.

planter   a person who makes a living by planting and growing crops, usually a single crop, such as cotton or tobacco.

plantain   a sort of small banana.

privateer   someone who robs another under a commission — with permission — from an enemy country. The robbery takes place at sea, or from ships.

prize   an item that has been captured, especially from a ship.

provisions   food and water.

quarter   allowing a person to live if he or she surrendered.

rack   an instrument of torture that stretches the victim's arms and legs.

ration   a set portion of food or water allowed to a person. Rationing often made small amounts of provisions last longer.

recompense   compensation given to make up for some sort of loss.

rigged   equipped with sails.

sail   describes the number of ships they had in all, not the number of sails all of the ships had.

sea tortoise   turtle, called *Tortuga de mar* by the Spanish.

shot   ammunition.

slave   a person who was bought and sold as property.

swine   pigs.

Tropic of Cancer   a line running parallel to the equator, but 23 1/2 degrees north of it.

try   to put on trial.

unanimously   with the agreement of everyone.

unleaven   bread made without any yeast-like substance to make it rise. It is flat and hard, more like a biscuit.

West India Company   a trading company set up to make money from trading in the West Indies. Several European countries had their own West India Companies: Britain, France, Spain, and Holland. There were also East India Companies, which traded with China, India, and the Spice Islands.

yams   a sort of potato, much sweeter in flavor than ordinary potatoes.

Index

Numbers in *italic* type refer to captions; numbers in **bold** type refer to information boxes.

Selection and additional material
© Heinemann Educational 1993